What's it like to be a...

HOME BUILDER

Written by Kira Daniel
Illustrated by Dick Smolinski

Troll Associates

Special Consultant: Louis J. Salierno, *Executive Vice President of Meridian Construction Company and Overlook Builders, Inc., Ramsey, New Jersey.*

Library of Congress Cataloging-in-Publication Data

Daniel, Kira.
    Home builder / by Kira Daniel; illustrated by Dick Smolinski.
      p.   cm.—(What's it like to be a...)
    Summary: A young boy watches as construction workers, carpenters,
roofers, plumbers, electricians, and other workers build a house.
    ISBN 0-8167-1420-7 (lib. bdg.)   ISBN 0-8167-1421-5 (pbk.)
    1. Construction workers—Juvenile literature. 2. Building—
Juvenile literature. [1. Construction workers. 2. Building.
3. Occupations.] I. Smolinski, Dick, ill. II. Title.
III. Series.
TH159.D36 1989
690'.023—dc19   88-10354

10 9 8 7 6 5 4 3 2 1

What's it like to be a...

HOME BUILDER

Cab

Scrap
Barrels

Pickup
Truck

Site Marker

4

Dump Truck

Bulldozer

Radiator

Blade

Crawler Tracks

Hydraulic Jack

Early one sunny August morning, construction workers arrive at an empty lot. Soon people are talking. Machines are moving. Truck motors roar.

Bulldozer

Exhaust Stack

Diesel Engine

Rad

Cab

Fuel Tank

Crawler Tracks

A truck screeches. Out jumps a tall man wearing a hard hat.

Pickup Truck

Toolbox

Site Plan

He checks to see which workers are there.
Then he notices a boy in a striped shirt watching
the workers.

"Hi!" says the man. "Do you live around here?"

"I'm Daniel. I live next door," says the boy. "Who are you?"

Van

Building Site

Building Stakes

Engine
Compartment

Radiator

arview
rror

Bumper

Headlight

"I'm a construction foreman," says the man.
"We're going to build a new house on this lot."
Daniel thinks about the big empty lot. It
seems hard to believe a house will soon be
standing there.

Bucket

Hydraulic Jack

Jointed [

Cab

Dump Truck

Bucket

Diesel
Engine

Backhoe

Drive
Wheel

Foundation Trench

"My name is Hank," says the man. "I'm in
charge of the workmen. You'll see some interesting
things happen here."

Hank points to a big digging machine. "Look!
That's a backhoe. It scoops up dirt with its big
bucket and pours it into a dump truck. The backhoe digs a deep hole for the foundation—the
bottom of the house. Would you like to sit in the
backhoe?"

Daniel grins. "You bet!"

"Fine," says Hank. "But wear this hard hat. It will protect your head in case you fall or something falls on you."

Daniel likes the hat.

Hard Hat

From high in the seat of the machine, Daniel can see all the construction workers.

When he climbs down, Daniel asks, "How will the house look when it's finished?"

Safety Roll Bar

Gearshift Lever

Floor Plan

House Plan

"Look at these plans," says Hank. "An
architect drew them. We follow her drawings as
we build."

From then on, Daniel visits Hank every day.
One day he sees a red-and-white striped concrete
mixer at the field. A man named Fred is pouring
concrete. He smoothes it out. Then he lets it dry.

Driver's Cab

Concrete Mixer

Exhaust
Stack

Concrete

Engine

Drive Wheels

Footing

"This is the footing of the house," explains Fred. "The whole house rests on the footing—just as your whole body rests on your feet!"

Shovel

Footings are often poured several feet under the ground to prevent frost from cracking the foundation of the house.

Wood Forms

Concrete Footings

Trowel

Concrete Block

Mortar Mix

Mortar Box

Mortar Mix

Another day, Daniel watches Fred build the foundation walls with blocks.

"I use cement mortar to hold the blocks together," explains Fred.

Daniel feels the mortar. It is smooth and sticky. He watches Fred's wall grow.

Mortar

Trowel

Mortar

Concrete Block

Stud

Wall Plate

Foundation Wall

Sill Plate

Footing

After a few days, Daniel meets Martha and Bill.

"They're carpenters," explains Hank. "They'll build the frame of the walls, ceilings, floors, and roof. The frame is like the wood 'skeleton' of the house. Then Martha and Bill will nail plywood sheathing to the outside of the frame."

Daniel likes to smell the fresh-cut wood. He likes to watch the carpenters work with their saws, hammers, and nails.

Roof Sheathing

Wall Sheathing

Frame

Power Saw

Plywood Stack

Tenpenny Nail

Claw Hammer

Early in September, school starts. Each day after school, Daniel goes to the house to see what has been added.

Scaffold

Air Vents

Wall
Sheathing

Extension
Ladder

Roofing Shingle

"Today roofers hammered shingles on the roof. Now water won't drip into the house when it rains," Hank tells Daniel.

Daniel feels one of the rough shingles.

21

Window Frame

Tar Paper

Siding

Nail Pouch

Foundation

"Also, carpenters put siding on the outside," says Hank. "We're closing in the house for the winter. Then we'll work inside."

Corner Cap

Daniel looks up at Hank. Hank seems to know everything about building.

One day Daniel sees many trucks parked outside the house. Inside he meets Ernie, the plumber. Ernie is putting in water pipes.

Water Pipe

Pipe Wrench

Foundation Wall

Val

Shut-Off Valve

Propane Torch

Crescent Wrench

Toolbox

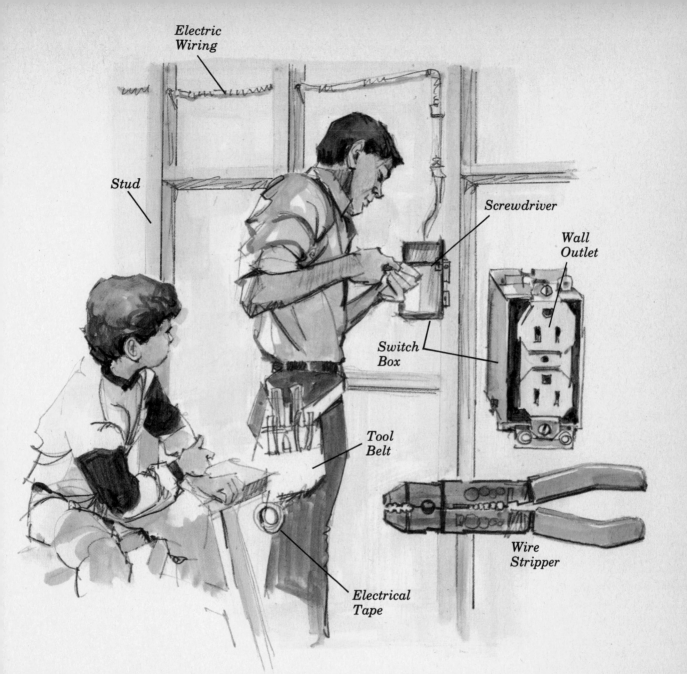

Electric Wiring

Stud

Screwdriver

Wall Outlet

Switch Box

Tool Belt

Electrical Tape

Wire Stripper

He meets Ken, the electrician. Ken is connecting wires.

"Soon we'll have electricity to turn on the lights," says Ken. He hums as he works.

Copper Water Pipes

Valve

Flue

Pressure
Tank

Furnace

Hot
Water
Heater

Burner
Motor

Daniel watches other workers put in the
heating system. Soon pipes and wires stretch up
and down through the house.

Eaves

Siding

Paint Can

Extension Ladder

Wall Brush

He watches painters paint. He sees red and
yellow leaves blow off trees around the field.
"Cold weather is coming," thinks Daniel.

One day icy snowflakes fall on the house. Daniel sees workers carry in plasterboards. Inside Daniel can't believe what he sees. Someone with huge "legs" made of metal springs is walking around. He is putting tape and Spackle over the joints on the ceiling.

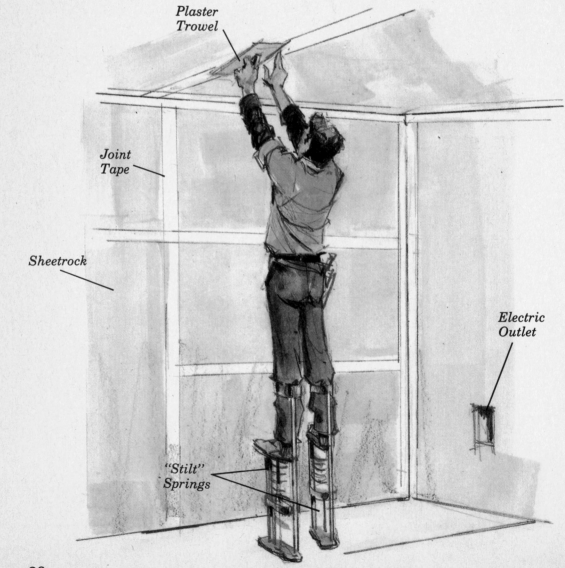

Plaster
Trowel

Joint
Tape

Sheetrock

Electric
Outlet

"Stilt"
Springs

Plywood
Flooring

"Meet Vito," says Hank. "The boards are called sheetrock. Vito uses sheetrock to make the inside ceilings and walls. He wears tall springs so he'll be able to walk around and reach the ceilings."

"Wow!" says Daniel. "May I try on the springs?"

"No," says Hank. "It takes a long time to learn to walk with them."

When winter comes, the ground freezes. But work goes on inside the house.

In the kitchen, workers lay a tile floor. In the living room, painters open cans of green paint.

"Would you like to help?" asks Tom, the painter.

He shows Daniel how to keep paint from dripping off the roller.

Painter's Hat

Bay Window

Coveralls

Roller

Paint Can

Paint Tray

Pickup Truck

Sapling

Water
Hose

Root
Ball

Spade

Nozzle

In the spring, bulldozers push dirt around the
house. Workers unload trees from a truck and
plant grass in the yard.

Daniel and Hank stand together and proudly look at the finished house.

"I wonder who will live in our new house," Daniel says.

"I don't know who will live here yet," says Hank. "But when I find out, I *will* tell them that one of my very best construction workers lives right next door."